A TRUNK FULL OF LAUGHS

1991 Henderson Publishing Limited

Illustrated by
Jon Haward

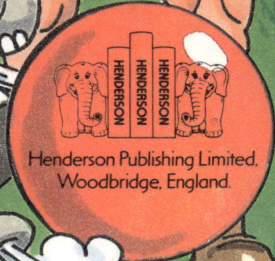

Henderson Publishing Limited,
Woodbridge, England.

WHAT'S TWELVE MINUS THREE?

I DON'T KNOW. I'M AN ADDER!

What's a hedgehog's favourite food? Prickled onions!

How do elephants dream? They phantasize!

When is the best time to buy a canary? When it's going cheap!

WHAT'S YOUR FAVOURITE GAME?

SNAKES AND ADDERS!

What's orange, hairy and has two wheels? An orang-utan on a bicycle!

What do you call a net full of fish? A load of cods!

What is a chimpanzee's favourite food? Gra-ape-fruit!

Why do elephants paint their toenails yellow? To hide upside-down in lemon trees.

MY SON HAS A JOB IN THE CITY!

REALLY? WHAT'S HIS LINE?

MONKEY BUSINESS!

SORRY I CAN'T CHAT! I'M A LITTLE HOARSE!

What bird doesn't sing?
A humming bird!

WHAT FAMILY DOES THE CHIMPANZEE BELONG TO?

I HAVEN'T A CLUE! NO ONE AROUND HERE'S GOT ONE!

An old lady went into a department store to buy some wool.
"I want to knit a coat for my dog," she told the assistant.
"How big is he?" the assistant asked her.
The old lady had great trouble deciding the size.
"Perhaps you should bring him in," suggested the assistant.
"Oh, dear, no!" said the old lady. "I want it to be a surprise!"

What breathes fire and hovers over ponds?
A dragonfly!

What snake will you always find on a car?
A windscreen viper!

STOP MAKING THAT NOISE!

I CAN'T, I'M A RATTLESNAKE!

A hungry horse had a sports car. What was its registration? *MTGG*

How would you describe an angry flea? Hopping mad!

WHAT IS THE CAPITAL OF HOLLAND?

HAMSTERDAM!

A PARROT CAN'T SWALLOW FISH.

NO, BUT A PELI-CAN!

What's got a beak, feathers and very long legs? *A duck on stilts.*

Two hippos jumped off a cliff! SPLASH! SPLASH! Don't you mean, BOOM! BOOM? No, they jumped into a *river*!

An old fly and a young fly settled on an old man's bald head. The old fly sighed, turned to the young fly and said, "When I was your age, this was only a footpath!"

DON'T SNAP AT ME!

Why does an elephant have wrinkly skin?
Because it would take forever to iron it!

Why couldn't the dog bark?
Because he was a bit husky!

When do chimpanzees itch and eat?
At the chimps' flea party!

A hyena won't roar,
He thinks that's a bore,
Or chatter like a chimpanzee,
He won't even croak,
He's not that sort of bloke,
But he'll laugh at a joke, you see!

What do you get if you cross a French Emperor and a crab?
Nipoleon!

What do cows cut the lawn with?
A mooer!

A CHICKEN WAS PLAYING IN A BAND. SUDDENLY, HE HAD TO STOP.

WHY?

BECAUSE HE LOST A DRUMSTICK!

What's the definition of a polygon? An empty parrot cage!

What do you call a baby donkey? An asset!

HAVE ONE OF YOUR ELEPHANTS BEEN IN MY LARDER?

HOW DID YOU KNOW?

FOOTPRINTS IN THE JELLY!

One morning, a man who had just moved into a new neighbourhood received a parcel that, in fact, was for someone else farther down the road. So he decided to deliver it, himself. He soon arrived at a house and rang the bell.

The owner of the house was out. But his talking parrot answered, "Who is it?"

"Your new neighbour with a parcel!" called the man, from the other side of the door.

"Who is it?" repeated the parrot.

"Your new neighbour with a parcel!" repeated the man.

"Who is it?" asked the parrot again.

"Your new neighbour with a parcel!" replied the man, becoming more and more exasperated.

"Who is it?" said the parrot, yet again. So the man answered once more. This went on for a full hour, until the poor man became totally exhausted.

"Who is it?" said the parrot for the umpteenth time.

"Your new neighbour with a parcel!" yelled the weary man through the letterbox. Suddenly, he collapsed with exhaustion. As he lay in the porch, the owner of the house returned and saw him.

"Who is it?" said the owner.

Just then, the parrot piped up, "Your new neighbour with a parcel!"

If a cat had eight legs, you could call it an octopuss?

What's the definition of a slug? A homeless snail!

A family of four elephants was going on holiday. When the taxi arrived to take them to the airport, the taxi-driver was puzzled. "How will I get you all in my car?" he asked.

"Easy!" said one elephant. "Two in the front seat, two in the back and our trunks in the boot!"

Why was the cockerel upset?
Because he was feeling hen-pecked!

A bee opened a theatre and was wondering whether or not to put on a Shakespearean play first. What did he say?
To bee or not to bee!

Why do elephants have yellow pads on their feet?
So they can't be seen if they lie upside-down in a bowl of custard!

A little bird visited the vet, and said: "I don't feel very well. Can you help?"
"Yes," replied the vet. "I'll give you some tweet-ment!"

What's dangerous and shoots out of trees? A squirrel with a pea-shooter!

What key won't fit in a lock?
A monkey!

What's pink, fat and waves a wand?
A fairy elephant!

DOCTOR, I'M FRIGHTENED I'LL BE SNATCHED BY A GIANT EAGLE!

YOU MUSTN'T GET CARRIED AWAY!

What animal should you never play games with?
A cheetah!

What do you call an elephant who keeps watching TV?
A telly-phant!

What do you call a cat that's accident-prone?
A cat-astrophe!

What's grey and goes round in circles?
An elephant in a tumble-drier!

HOW DID YOU LEARN TO SPEAK?

PARROT-FASHION!

What do you call an elephant that's taken a mud-bath?
A smelly-phant!

I'D STAY AWAY FROM HIM.

WHY?

BECAUSE HE'S A BOAR!

A horse decided to go into town. He saw a posh hotel and wanted to stay there.
"Have you a room for me, please?" he asked the receptionist.
The receptionist could hardly believe his eyes. "I don't think I would have one that's suitable for a horse!" he said.
"Of course you have" said the horse. "Give me the bridle suite!"

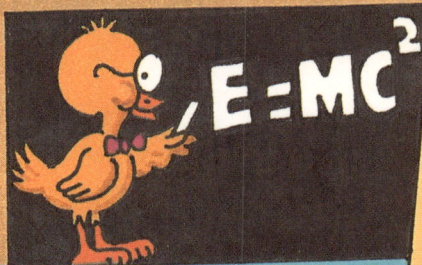

What is juicy, has prickles and four legs?
A porcupineapple!

A man walked into a hotel carrying a pet skunk.

"I'd like a double room, please," he said. The receptionist took one look at the skunk and held his nose. "But what about the smell?"

"Oh, the skunk doesn't mind at all!" replied the man.

Do you know the difference between an elephant and a biscuit?
Ever tried dipping an elephant in your tea?

What is a cat's favourite TV programme?
'Mews at 10!'

Picture puzzles! What are they?

Three elephants sniffing a sandwich!

Four mice having a conference!

Photograph of a giraffe — taken too close!

What travels underground at 100 miles per hour?
A jet-propelled mole!

MY PIG'S GOT NO NOSE

HOW DOES HE SMELL?

AWFUL!

In what plane do elephants like to fly?
A jumbo jet!

Why do elephants make good musicians?
Because they're great trumpeters!

What is a 'butter mountain'?
Two goats riding piggyback on an elephant?

What food swings through trees?
Monkey-nuts!

I'M HAVING A PARTY. WILL YOU BLOW UP ALL THE BALLOONS?

WHY ASK ME?

A little mouse gazed up at a bull elephant and gasped. "My, what a massive great thing you are. You're just HUGE!"
"Yes, replied the elephant loftily. "And you're such a poor, puny little thing, aren't you?"
"I know," sighed the mouse. "But I haven't been very well!"

BECAUSE YOU'RE A PUFF ADDER.

What do you call a hippo that is feeling very pleased with itself?
A happypotamus!

WHAT'S THE ABOMINABLE SNOWMAN'S FAVOURITE FOOD?

What animal works very hard?
A beaver!

SPAG-YETI!

EEECK!

What wallows in mud and squeaks?
A hippopotamouse!

Why did a parrot and an owl keep quarrelling?
Because the parrot called the owl a 'twit' and the owl kept replying, "Twit-to-you!"

An elephant walked into a baker's and asked for a dozen buns. The assistant froze on the spot and just stared, unable to speak.

"What's the matter with her?" the elephant asked a second white-faced assistant.

"W . . . we don't see elephants in here, v . . . very often!" quavered the girl, nervously.

"I'm not surprised," snapped the elephant, "when you're such a long way from the bus stop!"

What does a potato and a spider have in common?
Neither of them can fly a plane!

DID YOU HEAR ABOUT THE THIEF WHO TOOK HALF A-POUND OF ALMONDS, HALF-A-POUND OF BRAZILS AND A BAG OF PEANUTS?

SOUNDS LIKE A NUT TO ME!

GROOGH! I'VE JUST FOUND A MAGGOT IN MY APPLE!

CHEER UP! HALF A MAGGOT WOULD BE WORSE!

WHAT GOES RED, YELLOW, GREEN, YELLOW, RED?

A PACKET OF FRUIT SWEETS!

What is a queue-jumper?
A kangaroo on a billiard-table.

What do you do if you find an elephant in your hammock?
Sling it somewhere else!

What do you get if you cross an elephant and a kangaroo?
Big potholes all over the outback!

"I'm worried about my pet chimpanzee," its owner told the vet. "It keeps banging itself on the head with a clenched fist."

"Leave him with me," replied the vet. "Come back for him in a few days."

So the owner went away feeling very relieved. When he returned, he was delighted to find that the chimpanzee was cured.

"How did you manage it?" the owner asked the vet.

"Simple," replied the vet. "I gave the chimp a big mallet. He hit himself so hard that he lost his memory and quite forgot ever to do it again!"

Why can't two elephants go swimming at once?
Because they only have one pair of trunks!

What did the earwig say as he fell off the wall? *"Earwig-o, earwig-o, earwig-o!"*

WHAT MAKES YOUR EYES WATER AND JUMPS IN THE AIR?

A SPRING ONION!

What do you get if you cross an elephant and a sheep?
An outsize woolly!

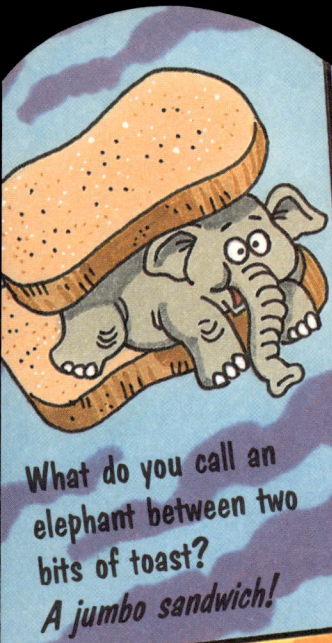

What do you call an elephant between two bits of toast? *A jumbo sandwich!*

Why is an elephant big, grey and wrinkly? *Because if it were small, round and white, it would be a ping-pong ball!*

What roars and swims underwater? *A sea lion!*

A conjurer who was entertaining on a cruise-liner always employed a chatty talking parrot in his act. Polly would make the odd amusing remark. "This evening, I shall perform a most unusual illusion," announced the conjurer. At that moment, the ship's boiler blew up, after which the parrot was next seen floating by on a piece of wreckage in the sea. The dazed conjurer was clinging on wearily beside him, while the parrot squawked, "I've seen some stupid tricks in my time, but . . . !"

What do you call a herd of elephants in a water-hole? *Swimming trunks!*

WHO LIVES IN THE DESERT AND WRITES PLAYS?

SHEIK SPEARE!

DOCTOR, DOCTOR, I KEEP THINKING I'M A GOAT!

WHEN DID THIS START?

WHEN I WAS A KID!

YOUR DOG CHASED MY HUSBAND ON HIS MOTOR-BIKE?

IMPOSSIBLE! MY DOG DOESN'T OWN A MOTOR-BIKE!

Who wrote the book: 'Into the Lion's Den'?
Hugo First.

WHAT'S SMOKED THEN HUNG ROUND YOUR NECK?

A KIPPER TIE!

What is fierce, striped and lives in the garden?
A tiger-lily!

Two elephants went to a fair. "Let's ride on the merry-go-round!" said the first. "They make me dizzy!" said the second. "You go on and I'll watch!"

So the first elephant agreed. But after a moment or two, the merry-go-round went out of control. It spun faster and faster, until the elephant was thrown off.

"Are you hurt?" cried the second elephant, hurrying up.

"Of course I am!" replied the first elephant, rather shaken. "I went round five times and you didn't even wave!"

What goes woof, tick, woof, tick?
A watch-dog!

What's lethal and lives underwater?
The codfather!

Why did the elephant put corn in his shoes?
Because he was pigeon-toed!

Did you hear about the cat who wanted to be a doctor?
He worked his way up from being a first-aid kit!

"Dad, dad, I've just seen a cow fall down!" said a little boy, anxiously.
"Don't get upset," replied his father. "It's no good crying over spilt milk!"

DOCTOR, DOCTOR! I KEEP THINKING I'M AN ELEPHANT?

NOW I'VE HERD IT ALL!

Why did the cockerel laugh at the chicken?
Because it told a cracking yolk!

What horses have the shortest ears?
The smallest ones!

If a black cat crosses your path, is it good luck?
Not if you're a mouse!

What's the hardest thing about learning to ride a horse?
The ground!

Who wrote the book, 'All About Dogs'?
Al Satian.

A herd of cows had formed an orchestra. What were they called? Moosicians!

What's brown, hops and is found in Greenland? A lost kangaroo!

If pigs flew planes, what would happen? Ham would go sky-high!

Patient: "Doctor, I keep thinking I'm a pony!"
Doctor: "I'll give you something to make your condition more stable!"

A grizzly walked up to a deer and said, "You've lost an antler!" When the deer went to look at his reflection in a nearby stream, he saw that his antlers were still there. The grizzly returned and told the deer that it had lost its tail. The deer swished it and found it was still in place. "Why do you keep on telling me things that aren't true?" the deer asked the grizzly. "I can't help it!" replied the grizzly. "I'm a bear-faced liar!"

What's the biggest ant in the world? A giant!

BOO!

NOT YOU AGAIN! YOU'VE BEEN TO MY SURGERY EVERY DAY FOR A MONTH!

I CAN'T HELP IT, DOCTOR! I KEEP THINKING I'M A DOG!

WELL, YOU REALLY MUST STOP HOUNDING ME!

What is a sheep's favourite sweet?
A chocolate baa!

Who wrote the book, 'Prehistoric Birds'?
Terry Dactyl.

What bird always jeers at you?
A Mockingbird!

If an elephant goes for a run and ends up out of breath, you could call him an elepant!

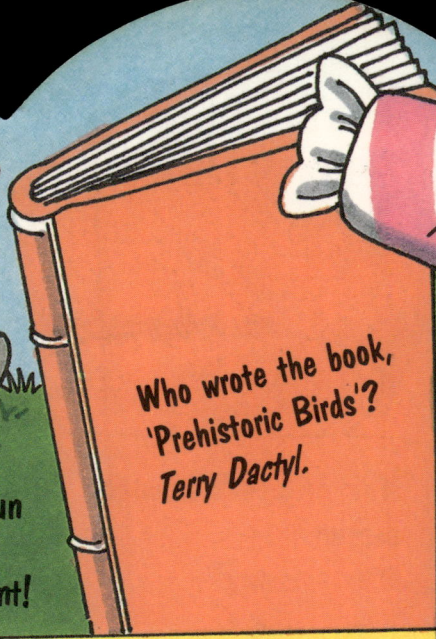

If a pig were crossed with the Tower of Pisa, what would you end up with?
Lean bacon!

What's small, green and highly-explosive?
A frog with a stick of dynamite!

What lives under the sea, has ten arms and is quick on the draw?
Billy the Squid!

WHAT DO YOU GET IF YOU CROSS AN EGYPTIAN HAT AND A TOP MODEL?

NOT JUST A PRETTY FEZ!

What hops about down under and buzzes? A wallabee!

A skunk was sleeping by the river, with his tail hanging in the water. Suddenly, a huge fish came up and seized the skunk by his tail. "I've caught him," thought the fish, "hook, line and stinker!"

CAN YOU KEEP A SECRET?

OF COURSE! MY LIPS ARE SEALED!

Knock, knock!
Who's there?
Gibbon!
Gibbon who?
Gibbon the chance I'd like to come in!

What do you get if you cross a kangaroo with a hippo? A hopopotamus!

HOW DOES A FOX KEEP HIS HOME CLEAN? WITH HIS BRUSH!

What bird is always playing around? A lark!

What wriggles, has no legs and enjoys visiting the library? A bookworm!

WHAT ROARS AND CAN BE FOUND IN A FLOWER-BED?

A SNAP DRAGON!

DID YOU HEAR ABOUT THE KANGAROO WHO MARRIED A POLAR BEAR?

YES. THEY HAD A LITTLE POLAR-NECKED JUMPER!

WHAT HAS A VERY LONG NECK AND FLOATS?

A GIRAFT!

Why did Miss Muffet run away from the creepy-crawly?
Because 'e spied 'er (spider)!

Knock, knock!
Who's there?
Cook!
Cook Who?
It must be spring!

WHAT DO YOU CALL A COWBOY WITH INDIGESTION?

WILD BILL HIC CUP!

What carries passengers and has lots of humps?
A camel train!

What tree gallops?
A horse chestnut!

What wears a cloak, visits granny in the woods and goes, "Oink, oink!"?
Little Red Riding Hog!

It was very hot on the African plain, but a lion was keeping cool thanks to a herd of elephants, who were flapping their huge ears all around him.

When a hot leopard arrived, he asked the elephants to keep him cool, too. But they refused. "How come they won't flap their ears for me, but they will for you?" the leopard asked the lion. "Simple," replied the lion. "They're my fan club!"

Who wrote the book, 'Tropical Fish'? *Barry Cuder (Barracuda).*

What do you call an animal with two heads, five legs and a prickly tail? *Ugly!*

What do you get if you cross a giraffe and a cow? *Very tall milk-shakes!*

An ostrich saw an egg that a budgie had layed. "I've never seen an egg that is so small!" he told the budgie. "I'm not surprised!" replied the budgie. "Usually, you've got your head in the sand!"

Knock, knock! Who's there? Aunty! Aunty Who? Aunty Lope (antelope).